GROW
IT NOW!

The Business Leader's Handbook to
Driving Revenue, Engagement,
and New Opportunities

By

Drew Aversa, MBA

INTRODUCTION

Entrepreneurship is the backbone of our American culture. The hours invested, challenges endured, and eternal optimism of our entrepreneurial spirit continues to create numerous opportunities for our society.

Given my background working in small business to Fortune 500, and traveling the globe meeting business leaders across industries, this handbook offers business leaders numerous resources to grow their business, teams, and reach.

Through the following chapters you will learn, how to: lead with purpose, grow your sales, develop your talent, market your brand, leverage new technology, and build emotional intelligence to effectively manage a multi-cultural and multi-generation workforce. Overall, you'll receive numerous insights into tools, tactics, and strategies to help you achieve your desired outcomes.

Whether you're starting your first business or you're a seasoned corporate leader, there is something in this book for you!

Beyond the practical advice offered, I believe that through our collective purpose as business leaders, we have the gift of making a profound impact in each of our communities through the value we create. Beyond profit, we are changing lives as we create economic opportunities across the globe in our connected world, if we harness business as a force for good.

You and your business matter...

May you live your purpose and take action to Grow it Now!

CONTENTS

ONE

DEFINE YOUR PURPOSE

"Without continual growth and progress, such words as improvement, achievement, and success have no meaning."

- Benjamin Franklin

The level of disruption across industries today is happening at a record pace. That's why it's critical that business leaders know how to grow their business, and how to Grow It Now!

As a business consultant and advisor on executive committees, I've worked with numerous industries ranging from: retail, construction, healthcare, government, hospitality, international trade, food and beverage, start- ups, non-profits, and more. My exposure to so many different kinds of businesses, management styles, and leaders is why people ask me -Drew, what's the one thing that stands out to you that applies to businesses in general? Well, the one thing always stands out is this, there are those in business who embrace innovation and there are those who uphold the status quo. In today's global, complex business environment, every business from large to small stands the risk of being disrupted if they are not in growth mode fueled by a *purpose driven* leadership team.

If you're ready to grow your brand, business, and impact, the following chapters will help you achieve your goals.

You can think about growing your business and doing the things you know need to get done to evolve, or you can take action and Grow It Now!

> *"Teachers Open The Doors,*
> *But You Must Enter By Yourself.*
>
> – Chinese Proverb

The action within us and within our organizations is largely what people call success. Success is made up of step-by- step movements towards our desired outcome(s); and in business, it also requires revenue – this is true across organizations from corporations to non-profits.

Seasoned non-profit leaders know that they need to think and act like for-profit companies to grow engagement, program effectiveness, and donor bases to secure revenue in the form of grants. Wall Street CEOs know that they need to show quarterly performance to retain shareholders while delivering value in the form of revenue growth as they drive new products, technology, or acquisitions. Small business owners who love their independence know that they have to create value for their local economy and treat people exceptionally well to retain loyalty as a destination of choice for consumers. Bottomline, every organization is dependent upon an exchange of perceived value to generate revenue to actualize the full potential of its resources to achieve growth.

Without revenue and positive cash flow, an organization is not sustainable and cannot grow; without a clear purpose or mission, many organizations struggle to define their place in the competitive business landscape which results in the business challenges many employers are facing today; and, without a sound human-centered business philosophy, companies lack the necessary employee engagement to drive their business forward. As Jack Welsh put it "There are only three measurements that tell you nearly everything you need to know about your organization's overall performance: employee engagement, customer satisfaction, and cash flow..."

Every industry from non-profits to Fortune 500 to small business is competitive. Competition drives change and change drives outcomes.

Today's consumers or clients have more choices available to them as a result of our online, hyper-connected society, so it is important that you know why you exist as the first pillar of your organization. Knowing **Why You Exist** will help you grow in every area of your business and it will help you attract the talent needed to grow it now!

Using the space provided below, I want you to answer this question – Why Does My Business Exist or Why Do We Exist?

WRITE

_____

_____

_____

_____

_____

_____

Great!

Now that you've listed why your organization exists, we are going to go a bit deeper...

Behind successful organizations are leaders who are clear in their own purpose, belief systems, and passion towards the mission of their company – this is the foundation of a healthy organization. A healthy organization derived from effective leadership also includes healthy revenue, attitudes, and culture.

> *"A company's culture is the foundation*
> *for future innovation. An entrepreneur's*
> *job is to build the foundation. "*

> – Brian Chesky

The defining difference between organizations that will sustain the rapid transformation we are experiencing and those that will not make it, is having a clear *sense of purpose*.

While there was a focus on organizational rhetoric using the term *sense of urgency* as a driver to spur CEOs into action amidst the realities of globalization, that term has also created some harm as it does not take into account the human condition and a human's absolute need to know their purpose.

If your mantra subscribed to a sense of urgency, I strongly encourage you to drop a sense of urgency today and adopt a sense of purpose as your new mantra; here's why...

Urgency, long-term is not sustainable and creates a stressful work environment that is not conducive to the health and wellbeing of your talent. Purpose, on the other hand, is sustainable and encourages a long-range mindset which is needed to survive and thrive. If you know your purpose, you don't need to react as often as cultures who focus on urgency do; you can let others react and patiently watch to see their outcomes, while holding true to your purpose in order to navigate things successfully in the storm.

Purpose provides clarity and the foundation necessary to grow.

Making your purpose clear allows those who resonate with your brand promise or culture to get engaged with your mission, from: brand champion employees to loyal vendors and those following you on social media.

Take a minute to build out why your business exists in greater detail. You may want to ask yourself the following as you write:

- What problem do we solve?
- How do we add value to people's lives?
- Who is our competition?
- What do we do better than our competition?
- What does our competition do better than us?
- If people could refer us, what would they say and who would they say it to?

- How is our business going to solve problems and stay relevant in the next 10 years?

Use this opportunity to take a moment to write down what makes your business valuable to the world today.

WRITE

_____

_____

_____

_____

_____

_____

Now that you've identified some of the key reasons why your business exists, it's time that we address the elephant in the room, FEAR.

Most humans have a level of fear that is healthy and that keeps us safe, yet some humans are filled with fear which keeps them stuck ruminating on things as the world of opportunity passes them by. Since business is a human led thing, it's important to understand our own fears as leaders because these subconscious or conscious fears can stop people from growing our business and they can keep people stuck in the status quo limiting the work they put in as they show up each day managing organizations.

Fear can be your greatest enemy or it can be your greatest teacher.

During my time in business school I traveled to India and learned a lot about organizational culture. Sitting through an executive seminar at Mahindra's headquarters, I was fascinated when I heard senior leaders share insight into their culture. I learned that Mahindra has a failure award that is presented annually to the team that has the biggest failure because they use failure as an avenue to drive innovation, creativity, and change. And for the record, they were clear that the leader of the team cannot get more than one failure award year after year.

In order to grow, you have to take a risk which is only possible if you breakthrough fear.

Something as simple as implementing new technology for founding members of established entities who are not comfortable using technology may cause fear based decision making, while competitors are implementing and training their next-generation talent on how to use technology to improve efficiency, sales, and customer service.

Depending on a leader's belief system and financial position, some leaders are more inclined to take big risks while others are risk adverse. Regardless, if you want to grow, what cannot happen is organizational paralysis analysis due to fear based cultures or fear based decision making processes.

While you are operating in a fear based mindset, your competition is operating in a strategic, innovative mindset that encourages failure, embraces challenges as learning opportunities, and loves to disrupt the bland status quo through engaging marketing tactics that drive growth. The choice is yours. If you want to grow it now, you cannot wait while the world passes you by. What will *you choose*?

To break-free from fear and its grip on your business, take a moment to write down every fear you have. List fears about your business, revenue, talent, competition, budget, future, and anything else, including your own lack of skills or knowledge in the area that requires evolution. Without breaking through fear, you can only grow so much. Now is the time to get real so you can get real results.

WRITE

_____

_____

_____

_____

_____

_____

_____

Great! Now that you've identified your fears across personal, professional, and organizational areas, it's time to go back to Why You Exist and how you can transform your fears into the action needed to *propel your purpose forward.*

As you develop clarity, take a moment to review your mission statement. Take the time to ensure your mission is still relevant today. For those starting a business, let's review some mission statements and the importance of having a stated purpose.

Mission Statement: These visible statements provide a clearly stated purpose of your business and the goals you have. A thoughtful mission statement can shape company culture, philosophy, and the focus of resources from talent to strategic acquisitions. Mission statements today must take into account the needs of present time and the not so distant future.

1. Uber: We ignite opportunity by setting the world in motion.
2. Google: To organize the world's information and make it universally accessible and useful.
3. Starbucks: To inspire and nurture the human spirit — one person, one cup and one neighborhood at a time.

While some organizations stop at mission statements, others create mission statements, vision statements, purpose statements, product statements, and more. Personally, I think most of what is needed can get done through a purposeful mission statement, which articulates precisely why you exist and what your value is long-term.

Take a moment to go over your mission statement.

WRITE

Your current mission statement:

_____

_____

_____

_____

_____

_____

_____

Your updated mission statement:

_____

_____

_____

_____

_____

_____

_____

Now that you have a clear sense of purpose for the mission at hand, there are three important things to grow your business – your *beliefs, attitude, and behavior.*

Our belief systems are complexed and made up throughout our lifetime as we digest information learned from our parents, media, friends, religious institutions, and the world around us.

The powerful saying, -*What we believe we become*| holds true in business.

As business leaders or entrepreneurs, we are the dreamers, the big believers, the disruptors, and the small batch of humans that remain restless in the status quo. This is a reason why we exist and why we are in positions of leadership. Our belief systems are rooted in an eternal optimism, success, and refusal to adhere to the status quo living a continuous quest to explore what's possible.

Every business leader, large or small, got here by some belief beyond the status quo.

Knowing this is imperative, as growth was founded in these healthy beliefs; and, the ability to grow is also founded in these abundance-grounded beliefs.

While some belief systems we inherited may not be healthy, it is ultimately up to us to define our belief systems as leaders to create the right culture and expectations needed to grow. Our beliefs will shape the next two important tools, our *attitude* and our *behavior*.

Our belief system is an ideology or set of principles that helps us interpret our everyday reality.

While we can sit in a room contemplating our beliefs like the ancient philosophers, action is needed to grow any organization, regardless of its size.

Attitudes drive the behavior needed to actualize our success. Our attitudes refer to our mental view rooted in our feelings or perceptions. Our attitude is often the subconscious stance that we take towards someone or something; that gut check that screams a sense of failure or a sense of opportunity.

In psychology, a key component of understanding our attitudes rests in understanding the two types of parenting styles that got us here.

Type 1: **The Critical Parent** - This parent has the attitude of distrust; a negative attitude. This can be seen in parents who freak out when their child wanders one foot out of their control causing the grown adult to lash out saying

-Child, get over here right now!

Type 2: **The Curious Parent** -This parent has the attitude of trust; a positive attitude. This can be seen in parents who trust their children and who give them the opportunity to explore the world around them with statements like -Hey, tell me what you see over there. Wow, that's cool. If you want to explore it further let me know and I will help you.

The two parenting styles are important because a lot of people are unaware, that as adults, people can carryon subconscious traits from their earlier years, if they were raised with a critical parent; and, if left unchecked, these inherited traits impact the workplace. Knowing what attitude you want to have is critical to knowing what kind of company you want to lead.

Attitude is everything when it comes to growing sales, teams, and health cultures.

Healthy people thrive in curiosity, clear communication, and uplifting environments. If you run a business with employees, this is important to reducing turnover costs and retaining your top intellectual property, *your talent*. If you are a professional services provider, the right attitude will also help you retain and attract more clients who feel a rush of fresh air doing business with you.

Our attitudes influence our behaviors. Our behaviors are the way in which we act of conduct ourselves towards others. While behavior can be influenced by hormones or other biological reasons, for the purpose of this audience, we will assume our behaviors are either learned or hardwired. Some behaviors are rooted in instinct and others like learning how to teach people to treat us are gained through the school of life.

> *"It's not what happens to us, but our response*
> *to what happens to us that hurts us."*
>
> – Stephen Covey

Business is stressful, challenging, and complex; however, with the right belief system, attitudes, and behaviors, we can take the necessary steps forward to grow. As business leaders, we have the ultimate choice to accept defeat or re-group to form a new strategy for victory.

No matter what happens, keep moving forward, keep a positive attitude, and treat everyone on your path with respect.

Take a moment to check-in with yourself on a personal level to evaluate these three key areas of leadership success.

WRITE

What are unhealthy beliefs that are impacting my leadership potential?

_____

_____

_____

_____

_____

_____

What are my biggest strengths?

_____

_____

_____

_____

_____

_____

_____

_____

What are my biggest areas for improvement if I were given a
performance evaluation?

_____

_____

_____

_____

_____

_____

_____

_____

What action or behavioral changes are needed for me to actualize my full potential?

_____

_____

_____

_____

_____

_____

_____

After you've identified your beliefs, attitudes, and behaviors that are aiding in your success, it's time to ask yourself if you are 100% committed to your goal of growing your business now!

To remain committed to growing your team, your business, your revenue, and your success, you need to know what you are committed to and **WHY** you are committed. A reason for committing to working as an entrepreneur might be to earn an uncapped sales commission to take care of your family. Next, you need to know what the alternative choices are if you do not keep that commitment or if you break it so excuses to growth are not an option. The alternative to providing for your family as a driven entrepreneur is staying poor and struggling with bills month to month or working under a sales plan that lowers your bonuses, even when you crush it! Good! Now that you know what you are committed to, why you are committed, and what the alternative of not keeping that commitment looks like, combine these to make your *commitment statement* that you will look at every day when you wake up to drive your growth plan forward.

Example: I am committed to making a great life for my family and am committed to the right beliefs, attitude, and behavior to make this so ***because*** the alternative of staying poor is no longer an option for me as a responsible provider to my family.

Then, add this to the end of your commitment statement:

I know this can be done and I am committed to achieving this goal!

WRITE

Commitment Statement:

_____

_____

_____

_____

_____

_____

Having a clear sense of purpose and commitment will help you show up strong everyday as a leader who has the responsibility to inspire, motivate, and influence others towards the growth of your organization.

TWO

INSIGHT, TOOLS, AND TIPS TO GROW YOUR BUSINESS

"Focus on building the best possible business. If you are great, people will notice and opportunities will appear."

– Mark Cuban

Small businesses across the world keep our economies going as they support jobs, professional development, and local needs. From your quaint neighborhood coffee shop to after-school tutoring programs, small business ownership comes in numerous forms, industries, and sizes.

According to research, small businesses present pathways to entrepreneurship and independence, yet, at the same time, 50% of small businesses fail within five years!

The following tips are here to help small business owners showcase their value to help entrepreneurs thrive!

TIP 1 - Know Your Market and Be Exceptional in What You Do!

Consumers have numerous choices today given traditional brick and mortar retailers and online offerings that display product ratings from peers.

One of the most common things I hear from people when I consult is "We're better than our competition." While ego can move you forward as an entrepreneur, it won't keep your doors open when the reality of a competitive marketplace humbles you.

My advice, spend time on market research or hire a consultant to do some groundwork for you to know reality over fantasy.

Market research will help you identify who is already in your space, their strengths and weaknesses, what customers are saying on public sites like Yelp or Google reviews, check-ins to determine local engagement, and industry trends to know if you're entering a dying industry or one on the verge of disruption.

After you've gathered information on your market, start brainstorming on how you will be exceptional in what you do and how you will sustain that, which leads us to the next tip.

TIP 2 - Have a Solid Offering and Innovate Before You Die

Every brand has a solid offering to drive the bulk of their revenue. While Starbucks might offer a seasonal item like the famous unicorn frappuccinio, they do this to drive incremental revenue compared to the core of their business which is coffee. Whether you are a brand that centers around products or a professional services firm that centers around work products, you need to know what your core offerings are and focus on growing these to build a strong base to build upon.

While your core offering will drive the bulk of your business, you must innovate or you will place yourself and your company at-risk for being disrupted. For example, we witnessed the plight of taxi cab drivers, who once spent thousands of dollars to secure their futures with expensive permits go by the wayside as Uber and Lyft made it easy for anyone with a vehicle to start earning money. Cab drivers relied on the strength of their unions, in a time when union membership was declining, as their main bargaining chip to secure their jobs. This lesson teaches, that there is no guarantee of any business making it, but there is a guarantee of 100% failure in due time if you fail to innovate or adopt new business models before being forced out or forced to evolve.

Every industry today faces some risk for disruption and those who do not stay informed are at the highest risk for extinction. Spend time attending industry trade shows to learn what's going on so you can stay ahead of the curve because your future depends on it!

TIP 3 – Choosing Between Traditional or Online Environments to Showcase Your Offerings

One of the biggest expenses outside of employees is real estate. In my hometown of San Francisco, rents climb at astronomical rates making the pathway to entrepreneurship a lot more challenging, requiring start- up restaurateurs to know their product and above-average finance skills.

How you use your real estate or any brick and mortar application today is critical.

When I view a restaurant as a consultant, I view it as a manufacturing assembly line and take out the emotional service part for a brief second. You have a line of cooks churning out products for consumers who have an expressed demand. While assembly lines need downtime for maintenance, they need to be producing as much as possible. Retailers can use partnerships with companies like UberEats, GrubHub, etc. to increase production and sales to consumers who have a demand for their product, making it easier to order instead of having to dine-in. In this example, restaurant owners should also think about co-ops and space sharing if their operations do not warrant a larger space as the increase in urban real estate values drives higher commercial rents.

When building out your real estate, take the time to know what your revenue per square foot calculates. Know why you need your real estate and strategize on how to maximize the use of the space for present time and future needs.

In retail, the pinnacle of a lot of brands is to have storefronts to showcase their value and offer experiential product experiences. While this is a great goal, you can also showcase your value through online avenues minimizing the risk of expensive leases if things don't go as planned. Remember, the online environment is changing and will offer consumers virtual store experiences in the future, shifting costs from real estate into virtual reality or augmented reality technology shifting the purpose of real estate into a new dimension across many industries.

TIP 4 - Technology, Technology, Technology

Technology improvements are critical to shaping your business so that your operations are efficient, your customers engaged, and your leadership team members informed.

Technology comes in many forms from Salesforce.com which can help organizations improve process flows, real- time financial reporting, up-to-date customer info to Revel Systems which helps retailers at the Point of Sale to Google documents that can be shared to collaborate.

Understanding your industry, competition, and needs of internal and external stakeholders is the first step to thinking about what technology you need in your business.

At minimum, every small business today should have a clean website that is mobile friendly to integrate into Google search results so that they can tell their story to people who are interested in their business.

Beyond procuring technology, is the need to adopt buy-in to implement the technology with your teams.

Conducting workshops on business growth and team building, I ask senior leaders why they are reluctant to embrace technology; the number one answer is – *a lack of trust in the technology and then a lack of trust in their people.*

Unfortunately answers like these are why it took many organizations too much time to embrace remote work until they were forced to do so in the 2020 COVID-19 coronavirus pandemic.

Within days of the emergency orders surrounding the coronavirus, companies stopped all non-essential tasks, focused on the true work at hand, and got their teams set- up with the right technology tools to carryout out business from home; what was avoided for years was executed in a matter of days.

During this time, organizations surveyed their employees, and found: that many employees and leaders embraced this change giving up two hour long one-way commutes and using this time to focus on their families, fitness, or hobbies that were neglected as organizations avoided leveraging technology to create better employee experiences, and the choice to work remotely in the comfort of one's home.

Technology can be a great tool to live better lives while still getting things done as long as leaders have clear outcomes and focus on a business leadership philosophy that is outcomes driven and results driven, over micromanaging every coffee break their people take.

From a customer standpoint, the next-generation of consumers demand the need for technology, relevant information, and the ability to share their experience with your brand online via reviews or pictures. The next-generation of employees also demand technology as a tool to improve work-life balance with the goals of business productivity in mind.

From a financial point, shifting your mindset to embrace technology will also propel you to understand that data is today's new currency. The more data and real-time insights into your business, teams, and processes, the better equipped you'll be to respond instead of react.

Next, find a moment to research the latest technology that is available and relevant to your business by answering the following questions. This must be part of your strategic plan!

WRITE

What are three technology solutions that can increase your operational efficiency?

_____

_____

_____

_____

_____

_____

_____

What are three technology solutions that can increase the speed and accuracy of communication?

_____

_____

_____

_____

_____

_____

What are three technology solutions that can assist in managing revenue tracking and keeping track of your key relationships or loyal customers?

_____

_____

_____

_____

_____

_____

While not one solution solves every business challenge, try to find the best solution that integrates with third parties through APIs so you get more reach for the service you are paying.

If you are negotiating a technology deal for your business, consider the volume of payments run through the system, data you are sharing with the tech company (hint, hint, they may make money off of your data), and overall cost savings to your business with improved tracking of labor, customers, and real time insights so you can have a strong understanding of the mutual value of doing business with your chosen technology companies.

TIP 5 - Figure Out the Labor Challenge

Talent is what keeps companies energized! It also accounts for one of the biggest costs to any organization.

How you view your talent and the hours they labor are critical as a leader.

It's a tough world today when margins in a lot of small businesses are small and labor costs continue to climb in urban cores. Unfortunately, the average consumer does not care that your ingredients and employees cost more as they order their favorite ice cream expecting a reasonable price to satiate their sugar-fix; or, that when hiring against competitors, your small business is struggling to retain talent as the franchise next door offers 401K plans, healthcare, and paid time off making small employers a backup plan to many employees today. So, here you are, at the cross-roads of a public policy issue and upset customers who want more for less in today's Amazon bargain world and in a world where rising minimum wages makes it nearly impossible to maintain a healthy profit margin to ensure business sustainability in numerous industries and regions that are not aligned from a basic economic standpoint.

While every business owner gets this, employees are still demanding for more.

Sites like Glassdoor, review employers, and allow employees the opportunity to share their experiences on a public platform, similar to Yelp. As employees gain a stronger digital voice, it's even more critical for employers to take action on public policy issues that impact hiring, recruiting, retaining talent, and running profitable organizations.

Small business owners need to work together to solve these challenges through local Chambers of Commerce, and through regional collaboration in urban areas to figure out the workforce challenge today.

As a business leader, you have to figure out your labor challenge and create non-traditional labor solutions, co-op models of expense sharing, and creative approaches to attract and retain talent. The old attitude of simply providing a job doesn't cut it for today's informed workforce, despite the numerous challenges small business owners face today.

Whether you are running a big business or a small business, people are the backbone of how you grow.

Build a culture of purpose, develop your talent, invest in those who keep your dream alive, and network with other business owners to create solutions on a regional level that impact your bottom-line, from taxes to non-traditional approaches to co-op healthcare plans to reduce turnover costs.

Creativity is what got you here and creativity will keep your talent there!

BONUS TIP - Scale Your Business if You Can

Economies of scale help entrepreneurs reach more people at better profit margins. As you develop a plan to scale, take note of what systems you need, what vendors want to work with you to offer better pricing, what lenders are willing to give you money at the best terms possible, and what markets present the most reward for the risk you're undertaking.

Growth presents the opportunity for you to have more choices in who you do business with and where you do your business to make your impact.

While one market may run a certain way, we've seen case studies from giants like Home Depot fail in China to regional franchises declaring bankruptcy after growing too fast. That is why my advice is, *scale if you can.*

Knowing when to stay where you're at and when to grow is a challenge for type-A entrepreneurs who are driven by passion, optimism, and true grit. To know when it's time to scale, consider hiring a consultant in addition to putting together a free sounding board of leaders in your network to review your ambitious growth plan to improve your chances of success.

Remember, running a small business today requires a different approach to be sustainable for tomorrow.

Keep improving your offerings, innovative where you can, and enjoy the ability to change the lives of the people who work for you and who rely on you to provide a great experience each day. While you might be small in terms of business, the number of small business owners is massive, so get connected and keep it growing!

THREE

LEARN THE BASICS OF SALES VS. MARKETING

People tend to love marketing because it is fun, creative, and highly visible; yet, people tend to loathe sales because it is hard work, potentially awkward, and something 99% of business schools never teach business students. While you can have amazing marketing, polished stories, etc. you MUST have sales to pay your bills.

As a MBA graduate, I always thought it was ironic that most traditional MBA programs do not cover human resources management and sales, when these two are the backbone of any business throughout the world! While you can learn fancy finance skills, they will not mean a thing if you do not know the psychology and process of selling; and, without stable revenue, it will be very difficult to pay people wages required to keep talent committed. That said, here's why we take a look at the difference between sales and marketing, as I offer you my strategies to close deals and grow your sales.

First, you have to know what a sale is. In the olden days before currency, people bartered and traded goods that had a perceived value in an exchange – *the word exchange is critical, so never forget it!* Today, we have a stock exchange where people buy and sell stocks for a perceived value given market conditions and demand; we also sell commodity goods like coffee on indexes that take into account the market's interests using fundamental economic terms like supply and demand.

When you make a sale, you are providing a perceived value and you are conducting an exchange between buyer and seller in an amount deemed reasonable by both sides for that exchange.

If no one wants your product, you either have no value in the market, which is probably not the case, or, you need to re-define your value and price point to where it clicks. Remember, there is a market for everything, even if you can only sell to friends and family as you start – *they are still taking place in an exchange.*

The key to sales is having the right revenue coming in and the right frequency to maintain your operations; to grow, you also need to increase revenue and figure out ways to optimize profit margins.

Your mindset is everything when it comes to sales.

Everything from job interviews to negotiating with vendors to selling a hamburger or million-dollar mansion revolves around the psychology of a sale.

When most people meet, there is a brief period in time that their mind determines if you are trustworthy or not; this is rooted in our biology as a primal survival mechanism. As non-verbal communication accounts for most of how we communicate, you need to show-up strong because first impressions matter.

Prior to your first impression, take the time to do your research. Do you know:

1. What the person or loyal customer is interested in?
2. What a company's plans are after reading things like annual reports?
3. How your prospect markets and if there are potential opportunities to show-up together through social media to demonstrate the value of your partnership, product, or service?
4. Who they do business with already? Or, where they already shop and spend their money?
5. Who your known competitors are and who is also out there disrupting in your space? Don't forget, even the most powerful companies out there are prone to failure if they fail to evolve. You always have competition where capitalism reigns.

Before I meet with anyone, I do my research on the person I am meeting with, their company, and all available public information, because...

Bonding and rapport are critical to establishing a foundation of trust.

Next, I use the time together to build a line of communication that allows for an exchange of ideas, sharing valuable information, and follow-up interactions. The goal of sales is to earn repeat business because it takes a lot of energy to earn someone's business for the first time and a second to lose it if trust or expectations are broken.

Then, instead of pitching on products and features, which everyone is worn out on today, you need to present value, success stories, and the WHY, behind why people find whatever you are selling valuable, worthwhile, and worth spending their hard-earned money on.

VALUE is everything today!

While what you are selling may be highly technical, always lead with value over being in the weeds discussing how cool this valve is or how strong that piece of rubber is on that gasket.

Have a great story and remember, *people buy from people they know, like, and trust.*

Whether you are a buyer or a seller, you also need to have your no- go points made up and know when it is time to walk away from a deal, because not every deal is a good deal. In an ideal world, both seller and buyer feel the exchange is valuable. I always encourage the no-go approach with my food and beverage clients as they negotiate with vendors because there are a lot of choices out there. If you are running a business, do not feel like you are a victim; do your due diligence, get multiple quotes within reason, and see who backs you up when an order gets missed.

When negotiating, you can negotiate on an interest or a position. A position might be a hard number, whereas, an interest might take into account the vendor's desires to work with you on ensuring you are truly profitable, bringing in additional resources on-top of favorable pricing. Knowing your desired outcome and driving the conversation that way is a good starting point when negotiating to close a deal.

Beyond the basics of sales, you need to know what your target market is that you want to sell to and if there are any other channels that you can tap into with what you are already doing to drive incremental revenue.

This leads us to marketing...

The goal of marketing is to utilize the 7Ps to drive sales:

Product - an item that satisfies the consumer's needs or wants. Products may be tangible (goods) or intangible (services, ideas or experiences). Product decisions include the "quality, features, benefits, style, design, branding, packaging, services, warranties, guarantees, life cycles, investments and returns

Price - the amount a customer pays for a product. Price may also refer to the sacrifice consumers are prepared to make to acquire a product (e.g. time or effort). Price is the only variable that has implications for revenue. Price also includes considerations of customer perceived value.

Place - refers to providing customer access; direct or indirect channels to market, geographical distribution, territorial coverage, retail outlet, market location, catalogues, inventory, logistics and order fulfillment. Place refers either to the physical location where a business carries out business or the distribution channels used to reach markets. Place may refer to a retail outlet, but increasingly refers to virtual stores such as a mail order catalogue, a telephone call center or a website; place considers providing convenience for consumer.

Promotion – includes traditional marketing, direct promotion aka sales, public relations, and communication in addition to online needs, such as: search engine optimization (SEO), pay-per-click (PPC), reputation management to encourage positive comments, online partnerships leveraging third-party websites to promote products or services, interactive advertising, email marketing, and targeted social media campaigns leveraging consumer insight data for market segmentation to reach the right customers.

Process – includes the procedures, mechanisms and flow of activities by which service is delivered. This can include: human factors who participate in service delivery to promote a company's values to customers. Sites such as LinkedIn leverage employee engagement on the platform to promote company brands tied to their employees that are visible before the public.

Physical Evidence – is the environment in which service occurs or the space where customers and service personnel interact. A great example of this are Apple retail stores that provide a modern, minimalist, on-brand experience for their customers over a worn-out cell phone store. Physical evidence can include furniture, service counters, and abstract elements of design like color and layout of the space.

Performance – measures how well a company is doing in the marketplace and if it is reaching its financial goals. This is crucial, in that, marketers must work with sales leadership, finance, accounting, and the CEO to ensure what they are producing is driving the desired performance.

Overall, marketing and sales go hand-in-hand. A great salesperson needs strong marketing support to reinforce what they are trying to accomplish, providing an exchange of value. Marketing needs to leverage the human intelligence from the sales team to continuously refine value propositions, advertising, and the customer experience to stay relevant.

Relevant marketers know the importance of experiences and how experiential marketing can drive revenue.

Putting this intro practice, we'll use an actual case study of a project I consulted on:

CASE STUDY

When I worked with the Ashland Schools Foundation to grow their annual Monster Dash Run for Education, I developed a strategy that took that run from 300 runners to 1000 runners in one year – from a sales standpoint, this was a revenue lift in the form of paid event registrations. From an experience standpoint, I added online registration with a friendly new website and chip timing to provide runners real time results. I also created a pre-race pasta party with a silent auction and live band, so that non- runners who support education could participate making this inclusive to the entire community. To increase brand equity for the run, turning it into a regional event, I negotiated corporate sponsorships in exchange for products and to cross-market the event, giving corporations something positive to market showing their impact in the local community. Since, the event has raised over $150,000 because it added value, innovated, and provided ways to engaged donors, aka customers, in addition to runners. Using this example, see if you can identify what was used from a marketing standpoint to grow this race, using the Ps above.

_____

_____

_____

_____

Whether you are selling frozen yogurt or selling to the C-suite, which both I've done, these principles apply. You need to understand your customer, connect with them, provide value to them, drive performance, reinforce the value of their exchange with you, and earn repeat business as your marketing team strives to stay relevant and reach customers across multiple channels in today's physical and online business environments while retaining a solid customer base.

If you need more help on marketing and sales, remember, I am just a phone call away if you schedule a call with me on my website www.DrewAversa.com today!

FOUR

KNOW THE DIFFERENCE BETWEEN STRATEGIES AND TACTICS

Firefighters save lives because they know the difference between strategies and tactics. Not understanding these differences can mean the matter of life and death; in business, it can mean the matter of working in your business with your head to the grindstone or working on your business from an elevated position to see the whole picture, both offering different results.

On the fireground, strategies are the what of what needs to get done overall, e.g. put the fire out safely and return everyone back to their firehouses in one piece versus tactics, which are how things get done, from pulling the right hose line to cutting a hole in a roof to let the hot air get out. Strategy is the large-scale general plan, and tactics are the ways of implementing the strategy. Strategies can also be offensive, where firefighters enter the building aggressively because the stakes are high to save a potential life, or they can take a defensive action surrounding the building with water to put the fire out if the building is deemed a loss with no life hazard. In these instances, command staff, or in civilian terms, fire executives, make decisions that impact the outcome of the incident, be it a small fire or large wildland fire raging for weeks.

In business, people often refer to strategy as the 30,000 foot view that a pilot sees as they strategically navigate the jet stream high above the clouds finding the optimal route to their destination; at the same time, pilots also have checklists to ensure the tactics they use to get from point A to point B are done in the right steps.

In business, knowing where you want to go and knowing how to get there, ideally happen in sync if leadership is effective.

A rudderless organization is often noticeable when circular conversations are taking place; essentially, where no one seems in charge, yet many have titles alluding that they're in charge. When people are confronted in organizations like this, they fail to know the step-by-step tactics necessary to execute the overarching strategy. Worse, if a company does not have a strategy, people are left with outdated tactics which cost time, money, and resources as they try to put out so-called office fires with out of date equipment.

Strategy requires that you know the full capabilities of everything on your chess board; when and how to move resources, in an efficient and effective manner that gets the job done.

Having the right tactical approach, from operating checklists to technology tools and how-to guides for staff, can help you free up time to get out of the weeds and back into overseeing your business.

When you work in your business, you are an employee, essentially. When you work on your business, you are a consultant, offering a high-level perspective of your organization's current state as you evaluate opportunities, threats, and areas for growth.

Fire Chief's don't run into burning buildings for a reason. They stay outside in full view of the building on fire at their command post that has every resource identified; they know how much water is flowing from what water mains, how many people are inside the building, and how many resources are available in the city should another large scale incident break out at the same time. What do you think would happen if the senior most leader was stuck inside the building, unable to see, and another big incident occurred at the same time requiring their presence to coordinate resources? It would not be good!

As a business leader, you can reduce so-called fires if you think strategically and allocate enough time in your schedule to pull back from tasks. Use this time to shadow your employees to see what resources they need, how their projects are going, and genuinely engage with them to find out what support is needed to win. Use this time to re- vamp your marketing plan, review what's trending on social media, and reassess if your strategy is still relevant as the competitive landscape changes.

Lastly, know what your defined objectives are to achieve your strategy. While goals are great to have, they are often too loose because they do not require action. Objectives, on the other had require action, commitment, and can largely be measured.

Measuring progress, tracking key performance indicators of success, and knowing where you're headed is vital if you want to grow it now!

FIVE

STARTING YOUR OWN BUSINESS VS. BUYING INTO A FRANCHISE

There are numerous business models out there. Two common models are that of starting your own business or buying an established business model, including franchises.

Franchising presents people the opportunity to invest in business models from restaurants to shipping services, and more. In 2017, there were 745,290 franchise establishments in the United States. While franchises make up large brands that people know, individual or multi-unit operators work hard as small business operators tied to a larger franchise strategy. Taking the time to perform the necessary due diligence can let you know if starting your own brand is worth it, or if being part of an established brand with established operations is worth considering. The following tips can help you decide if franchising is a smart move.

1. What You Should Be Getting

Investing in a franchise can be one of the best moves of your life to gain financial freedom or it can wreck you. In addition to paying a franchise fee, a monthly or yearly percentage of revenue for brand marketing and improvements, build-out costs, and tenant improvements after the 5 year mark to re-fresh your space, you should focus your attention on this as an investment because there are many other choices you can make when choosing where to put your hard earned money or risk of borrowing money to make a dream come true.

One of the major benefits beyond brand recognition and a strong leadership team at the helm of the overall strategy, is buying power.

Food and other supplies are expensive. As a small business owner, your buying power for supplies is often limited to the places most solo-preneurs shop. A strong franchise will focus on distribution and buying power to improve profit margins, so you make more money, ideally, than having a burger joint on your own. When franchises operate in more than one state, it is important to ensure that suppliers can carry the same menu items to retain brand integrity at the customer level. Imagine having a great tasting hamburger bun in one state and a mediocre one in another. The goal with franchises is to have a repeatable process with the same quality.

Technology is also critical to a successful business operation. Systems like REVEL offer operators the ability to set enterprise menu items, inventory management, and ordering to keep stores running in addition to labor modeling. Franchises today must invest in technology partnerships at the enterprise level and offer individual operators great systems to run their businesses. If you don't see technology as a key piece of the offering, run. Tech is in and it is here to stay.

Coaching is also critical to help your business stay afloat. From mandatory human resources training to sales training, strong franchises offer strong support to the operator to ensure their success. Having a conversation during the discovery phase is a great way to see if this is truly a partnership or a way for someone to make $30,000 off of you with little interest in seeing your success. There are plenty of horror stories out there of franchise promises and little support, so ask the hard questions and trust your gut if it says walk away.

A good franchise is a good partnership.

Stability is key. It will take most operators anywhere from 2-5 years to pay off their initial investments depending on the model they choose. If you see this model as something that is not sustainable or threatened by similar fads popping up, think twice before investing. If you see the leadership team has not figured out their core concept, profitability, distribution, and brand promise, think twice or see if there's an opportunity to join their leadership team to provide the needed guidance if you believe in the brand concept enough for the long-haul.

Marketing that delivers results. You will typically pay a fee each month or year for marketing. The parent organization will hire marketers to help you open your restaurant, start a social media program, learn what offers and when you can offer them to drive sales, and support from the top with corporate programs, messaging, and targeted ads to drive engagement. If you look at their marketing program and know you can do it better, question the fee you are paying and if they can truly drive sales from their marketing efforts to keep your business going. On the local level, you need to engage your community as a business leader with the big brand name behind you. Local marketing has always worked to build a strong following of loyal customers because people like the product and they like you, for caring about their needs from school parties to non-profit fundraisers. You can also see if the franchise has a social responsibility program and match for funds donated to non-profits. Franchises of the future need to value social responsibility as a core pillar of their business model to connect with next-generation consumers.

Location, Location, Location services. Ideally you will want to have a sound real estate team or access to retail brokers who know the landscape and who will offer unbiased opinions. While the franchise should know what real estate plays are best for their brand based on market research and pro formas, you can also reach out to local commercial real estate representatives early on to put the word out to find the best locations. When you become more aware of how franchises work, you will see a trend of stores that always seem to operate alongside each other in strip malls. If you notice what works well for your competition, consider a similar placement for your location.

2. What's Your ROI?

Under franchise law, the franchiser cannot tell you how much you will make. Some may provide you with a range based on similar locations, but none will tell you what you can make. This makes it critical to ask the hard questions and to gain access to other operators to speak with them directly. A good program has no issue with putting you in contact with happy operators. When you meet with an existing franchisee operator, you can ask questions like:

- Tell me how the experience is going for you?
- What support is going well and what is missing from the program?
- Would you open another location or multiple locations with this program?
- Are you happy with the money you are making compared to the initial investment?
- Have your sales grown or decreased, and if so, by what percentage since you've opened?
- Can you give me a range of what you think I will make as an owner-operator after expenses, including loans, if I want to pay myself a starting salary of $85,000? Is this doable or do I need to lower my salary?
- When do you expect to be debt free and turning a true profit?

3. Where You Are in Life

Running a business is not an easy task. The ability to think like an employee goes out the window when your employees call out sick on weekends forcing you to drop everything or close your doors disrupting the business promise you've presented.

Financial issues must be resolved before taking on more risk. In America, small businesses fail at high rates after the 5-year mark. What this means is this...you took a loan out for your franchise business opportunity, you received sales revenue to cover the bills, five years later you paid off your debt while earning a modest salary, and the industry changed or the franchise group changed resulting in declining sales and a brand that was a fad.

Most people in the franchise business who are not buying themselves a job and who are true investors do so in stable concepts, and across a region, controlling an area as multiple-unit operators or exclusive franchisees for a state or county. This has its benefits because operators can share resources more efficiently and can close down stores that are not performing versus one store, as they have a portfolio to manage.

The systems in place within a sound franchise offer hardworking, customer focused people the ability to do well, provided they learn fundamentals of management, human resources, leadership, and business.

Overall, franchising can present numerous opportunities to business savvy individuals who are looking for the right support, a fun experience, and ability to serve people doing what they love. For more resources checkout the International Franchise Association and their annual conference to see if franchising is right for you. Ultimately, starting your own brand or buying into a franchise is up to you. Both require the right due diligence and required work to grow.

SIX

GROWING YOUR BUSINESS USING SOCIAL MEDIA

Social media is a powerful way for business owners to generate brand awareness in order to capture new leads, customers, and referrals. Social media is a key piece to every brand, be it a personal brand, legacy brand, or disruptive brand. Knowing what social media platforms are out there and how to use them is key to one's business strategy. If you're looking to grow your business, the following pros and cons of major social media platforms will give you an understanding on how to use social media to your advantage.

Facebook

Started by Mark Zuckerberg in 2004, Facebook has more than 1.63 billion active daily users. and multiple features that make this a key platform for any brand today.

PROS

1. Global platform
2. Targeted marketing and advertising given massive amounts of consumer data
3. A/B testing of ads to test your offering
4. Engaging covers allow video and storytelling to wow people from the start as they view your page
5. Community building through Facebook groups and customization, including private groups to differentiate your customer base, e.g. VIP or regular and albums for historical data or referencing
6. Events to engage a wider audience in targeted locations
7. Facebook live to create a sense of urgency and demand to drive exclusive offerings and product roll-outs
8. Storytelling leveraging videos and cross-marketing through linking to other brand partners
9. Invite your friends to like your page to begin creating a following on company pages
10. Customer reviews
11. Large database to search competition and view their strategy for competitive insight to build your own social media marketing plan - frequency of posts, types of posts (text vs. picture vs. video), content, type of engagement from customers, influencer use, paid vs. organic, etc.
12. Virtual timeline

CONS

1. Data privacy concerns and moral compass of leadership
2. Algorithms can change requiring new A/B testing of ads, ad copy, etc.
3. Requires the creation of a personal Facebook account to manage a business page
4. Facebook pages vs. places can be confusing to consumers and time consuming for small business owners with multiple locations to properly manage reputation
5. Ads can be expensive if you don't know your target market given size of pool to advertise

LinkedIn

Are you looking to connect with decision makers? If so, LinkedIn is the platform for you! With over 303 million active monthly users and 92% of Fortune 500 companies on this platform, LinkedIn features personal profiles of business leaders, managers, CEOs, elected officials, and more. While old school sales leaders spent hours cold calling on companies trying to reach the top, targeting the people you want to reach has never been easier thanks to LinkedIn...pending you deliver value and articulate yourself as a personal brand.

PROS Development of thought leadership

1. Extensive global database that is easy-to-search and filter to find the right people, organizations, and titles you desire to connect with, e.g. search: VP business development technology San Francisco

2. Ability to showcase your professional experience and portfolio beyond a resume to make it clear why recruiters would want to contact you or why someone would trust you for an introductory call

3. Referral network and messaging to make introductions

4. Testimonials that immediately display trust, results, and recommendations from people instead of waiting for the reference check

5. Professional groups to network with and exchange resources to grow

6. LinkedIn Learning and online content to evolve as a professional

7. Video and article creation to demonstrate leadership in your field with the ability to attach hashtags #leadership #consultant #speaker to be found by others well past the initial posting date

8. The #1 Business to Business platform and lead generation portal to grow your business top to top and close C-level deals

9. Ability to see who viewed your profile so you can connect with these people who are interested in you

10. East to track metrics on post views and engagement
11. Development of executive thought leadership and positioning as key person in your industry

CONS

1. Prefers native video files (must be less than 10 minutes) over YouTube links to drive online content sharing and videos with subtitles (which requires spending more money)
2. Writing styles have changed to favor short, choppy, algorithm friendly text to drive views
3. Some people do not see the value in the platform as evidenced by lower numbers of users compared to Facebook, yet, the users on LinkedIn tend to be more senior level and know the value in the platform
4. Advertising is expensive as this is primarily a B2B space

Twitter

The favorite communication channel of Donald Trump's White House, Twitter! This platform has 68 million monthly active users in the United States and 330 million worldwide. Twitter posts can go viral by news agencies and is a great platform for opposition speech, which drives a large number of views in our hyper-critical society. In a recent Pew Research article, data tells us that Twitter users are younger than the average American, more likely to be a Democrat, and the top 10% of users frequently include political tweets.

PROS

1. Doubling from its inception of 140 characters to 280 characters, Twitter is the platform to highlight how witty or direct you can be with as few of words as possible

2. Users on Twitter use R/T for R/T meaning they will re-tweet your post if you re-tweet their post, driving organic sharing

3. Hashtag central and short form media heaven! If there is an #earthquake you will know about it in seconds before news agencies craft their traditional stories. Searching for local issues and relevant news is easy to do on Twitter and will result in real-time info on trending topics

4. If brands are engaging in political advocacy on issues like climate change or ethical sourcing, Twitter can be a platform to tell the world your position statement in just a few characters

CONS

1. Most users rarely tweet, but the most prolific 10% create 80% of tweets from adult U.S. users

2. Limited text to promote or articulate value propositions

3. Highly polarized and political space which may damage

a brand before it has a solid reputation and reputation management strategy as Twitter aims to connect people with shared interests, i.e. they do not foster diverse thinking

4. Limited text to respond to negative comments

Yelp

The service economy is massive! From restaurants, bars, hotels, law firms, auto mechanics, public agencies, and more, Yelp is the place for people to leave their review. Maintaining a favorable online reputation is critical for businesses to professional services providers today as people review and recommend within moments of their visit. This chart from Yelp breaks down the industries their platform covers. To date, Yelp has over 192 million reviews! A high percentage of Yelp users in America are college educated with 50% earning $100,000 or more.

PROS

1. Transparent review platform that ranks at the top of Google search
2. Ability to tell your story as a business owner or firm and engage with customers
3. Photos can highlight top offerings in visually sensitive markets such as food and beverage

4. Transparent ability to defend your reputation and share your side of the story because the customer is not always right

5. Lead generation with new traffic often generated after reviews

6. Specials and check-in offers to drive business during slow times

7. Community events and Yelp Elite membership to try new places

CONS

1. Think twice before creating a page. Once you create a page, good luck trying to get it removed. Yelp, seriously needs to do better at reasonable requests to remove pages, which I'll leave at that...

2. Their sales teams are non-stop and will be pitching offers constantly once you create a business page

3. Yelp seems to have two kinds of reviewers, those who hate your guts and those who love you. Remember, 60-80% of human thought is negative depending on the study you read, so this platform allows unconscious, negative humans the ability to rant their life's frustrations publicly. The good news is that you can respond calmly and state your view of the situation which positions you as a reasonable and caring business owner

4. People can take crappy photos of your business or product to skew visual perceptions to potential customers, so make sure you create updated digital content to stay fresh

Instagram

Acquired by Facebook, Instagram is a visually-forward social media platform that is excellent for lifestyle brands, travel enthusiast, foodies, and the next-generation of social media influencers reaching millennial and younger consumers. Of the over 1 billion monthly users, 90% are below the age of 35.

PROS

1. Teens say Instagram stories are the best way to reach them to promote a new product or feature
2. Stories are the best way to reach people and to have them engage with your brand
3. Sales can be generated through Instagram as one can present a clean story with nice visuals to promote a product
4. Influencers can make money on this platform promoting products from companies who are interested in reaching their target customer to reduce acquisition costs through direct marketing
5. A picture says a thousand words. Instagram is the place

to arrange your images in a tasteful waterfall of cascading images, videos, and stories to wow your audience

CONS

1. Hashtag policies and view count policies can impact distribution of posts and there is no transparent communication in place to forewarn loyal advertisers of these changes and how they will impact reach
2. Some hashtags have been reported to be shadow banned aka censorship if algorithms perceive a violation of community standards
3. While this was the 2nd most downloaded app in 2018 in the Apple app store, new subscribers are being added, so reach is still limited for large international brands
4. Acquired by Facebook so things can change from the original intent

Snapchat

78% of Americans aged 18-24 use the app Snapchat, which also hosts 180 million daily active users. If your business is focused on developing the next-generation of loyal consumers, Snap is where it's at!

PROS

1. 1, Peer to Peer messaging

2. Engaging filters to keep youth on the app as they are heavily influenced by the selfie-culture

3. Less saturated than other social media platforms making it easier to stand out

4. An app to watch for the future as it holds the interest and trust of younger consumers

CONS

1. Expensive to advertise if you want special filters on peak times

2. Still growing with a younger customer segment that has less immediate spending power

Influencers: Bloggers, Podcast Hosts, LinkedIn Super-Connectors, Speakers

Did you know that everyday people get paid to promote products or services? While Hollywood takes millions to place a product or brand logo in a movie from things like Rolex watches to orthopedic parts in the hit show ER to subtly influence viewers, local brands are turning to local people who have large *social networks* to influence their offerings. In this section, we'll look at how and why you want to work with influencers to grow your reach.

First-hand experience

As a speaker, I get approached by people who want me to promote their event in exchange for a speaking slot because I have over 10,000 people on my LinkedIn network...remember the demographic of LinkedIn users

from above, most are senior leaders or decision makers. When a conference host invites me, they are seeking my reach to influence other senior leaders to attend or send their talent as a starting point for event planners to meet new people and to begin the courtship of building a relationship to ask for sponsorship money or the opportunity to plan an event. In this case, the exchange of value is an opportunity for me to elevate my brand speaking at a notable event and for that organization to elevate their presence before my network, who might pay money to attend. As an influencer, it is important to define your values and who you will and will not work with as people approach you, and, as a company, it is important to know the values of your influencers as they represent your brand publicly.

When selecting an influencer or if you are an influencer choosing a brand to work with, consider the following:

1. Are we aligned in our values and any political statements that might come back full circle? Have both parties done their due diligence ensuring their reputations are aligned?
2. What demographic are you trying to target? Can the influencer reach them?
3. How many posts and what type of post do you want the

influencer to do? Static image, video, direct endorsement with link, etc.

4. Is the influencer crafting the story? Well, you need to treat them like a professional advertising partner because they are doing just that, creating a story to reach the market they know and in a way to get them to take action. If you pay ad agencies, you need to start thinking of influencers in a similar optic.

5. How valuable is the influencer's platform and what's the right exchange? Money, product, experience, ongoing affiliate partnership?

Example: My platform has 10,000 people who are mainly decision makers and in business leadership roles. If I work with a hotel brand to promote their hotel, I will need to determine what brand of hotel and Star level I want to promote, what feature so it does not come across like a blatant sales ad, a link with my code embedded so my client knows how many people were driven to them by me, and cost/value determination. Getting down to numbers: let's say I post two organic posts that reach 3,000 people who travel and who can make a decision on where they want to stay. Out of that number, five book a hotel stay for three nights at an average cost of $200 per night, the hotel generates $3,000 in new revenue plus the ability to earn referrals from satisfied guests and visibility on the new customer's social media channels, called a mushroom effect. For something like this, the hotel may provide me a few nights accommodation when a room is vacant during low season which only costs them the direct cost of cleaning the room and a few meals at their cost, plus a few perks or experiences through the concierge so I can feature these experiences. So, for a hundred or so dollars, the hotel has the opportunity to earn revenue and new customers at a low cost when they work with an influencer who has reach in their target market.

Influencers are a great addition to your marketing strategy, and most are more affordable than you think, as the millennial generation favors experiences.

Google

Last but not least, and one of the most important, Google! When people search, they most often use a search engine to find what they are looking for, and Google ranks at the top. Google is important because this is where your business will rank when searched; if directly searched, the first and second pages will hold a valuable insight into who you are, what your business is about, and any reviews. The tabs on top will host links to images, videos, news, and general information about your business.

PROS

1. Ability to claim your business page and update critical information like hours, address, website

2. Your website link and phone number are easily accessible

3. Google analytics can be tied to your website so you can see where people are searching from, what they are looking at, and ways you can optimize your site and ads with the help of a professional

4. Before people get to Yelp, they will come across Google reviews, so make sure you respond to these reviews as well

5. When starting a business or deciding on what product to develop, you need to look at Google trends. You can type in the words you want to use to see what words are on the upward trend or decline so you have a name that is headed in the right direction. You can also use Google trends to customize ads on certain times of the year when people's interests are focused in a certain direction

CONS

1. When things get placed on the web, they are indexed by Google and can take a long time to get off. If something hits the web, while it may be taken down, consider that it is still floating around there somewhere

YouTube

Does your brand have a cool story that needs to be told? Are you a personal brand or professional services provider who is recognized by your industry? YouTube is a great platform to showcase your expertise as a speaker or to teach others the value behind a product from things like makeup to camera lenses to travel tips. YouTube creators have their own channels and sub-categories to make searching for relevant info a breeze.

PROS

1. Loved by young and old
2. 1.9 billion active users per month
3. Works across languages in today's global environment
4. Easy to share links that can be used across platforms
5. Public and Private hosting options to share protected content
6. Depending on reach, you may be eligible to place ads on your videos to generate more revenue

CONS

1. Top creators use quality lighting, microphones for good sound quality, and professional cameras for Vlogging which requires money
2. Trolls can bash people and bots can thumbs down

videos giving false perceptions on the quality of content. If you want your content to get out there, you need to keep it visible with the option for comments...this requires a reputation management strategy

Website

Businesses today need their own website, period. A website consists of a domain name like www.DrewAversa.com and a hosting platform to build-out your site like www.Wix.com or www.WordPress.com Your hosting and domain name will cost you around $200 total. While other sites rely on their own community, the importance of having your own website rests in your ability to control your messaging and the ability to create a loyal community through email marketing, which is highly personalized to reach those who you know are 100% committed to your business. Your website is also a great place for you to write content on a blog so you can share this content across social media sites, text messages, etc. to people who will read what you have to say because you are positioned as a leader. Trust is also higher coming directly from you! You do not need to spend thousands on a website if you are a small business or regional brand.

SEVEN

YOUR SOCIAL MEDIA ROADMAP

You're probably wondering by now, where do I start?

As a business consultant, I help business owners implement a social media system so they are successful. While you can create accounts on each platform, not knowing how to use them appropriately or what content to share on each platform will inevitably result in time and money wasted. The key to a successful social media presence and strategy is to think of this as an interconnected system within your business instead of individual tasks to create better outcomes.

Now that you are ready to get onboard or grow your social media presence, it's critical that you take the time to create a content calendar and understand why content is so important in today's digital world. If you haven't looked into technology solutions that make posting easier, checkout Hootsuite before you craft your next post.

Here's why being consistent on social media matters...

Headlines make and break people every second in today's digital era. If you're at the older end of the millennial bracket like me, you may remember going outside to pick up the newspaper for your parents, and if you're older than me, you might even recall the era of newsboys yelling, -Extra, extra, read all about it!꘡ Emblazoned on that printed newspaper was a bold headline that spurred raucous debate from corporate offices to local watering holes.

While news formats have changed from when Johann

Carolus launched the first newspaper in 1605 to today's career-defaming tweets and real-time reporting by the public via Facebook Live, what hasn't changed is the power of a strong headline to capture the world's attention, setting one news channel above the rest on the same topic.

In business, you need to think about how your newspaper headline can differentiate your company from the rest.

To do this, start thinking about each month as a key topic to focus your social media marketing efforts. A 12-month headline plan might look like this:

- **January**: Launch a new product to drive this year's sales, giving your clients lead time.

- **February:** Reinforce the value of your current products via testimonials and data.

- **March:** Drop a line about your next best offering to stay interesting.

- **April:** Spring is here, and it's time to spring into action with your best offering.

- **May:** How may we help you? Send a reminder about customer experience and service.

- **June:** Focus on leadership and bringing in top talent once your budget is done.

- **July:** If you're an American-based company, highlight your Americana around the Fourth of July.

- **August:** It's back to school. Highlight how your company helps students and working families.

- **September:** Remind everyone that there's still room to engage with you before year's end.

- **October:** Have a foundation? Consider showcasing it.

- **November:** Get sentimental and show your vulnerable side. If you don't have one, get one.

- **December:** What's your year-end headline?

From there, you can build out a content calendar with daily and/or weekly content that is aligned to what you are trying to communicate that month. And, as each year comes to an end, I encourage you to think about your year- end headline. What is your top accomplishment for the year? Next, do this:

- Create the boldest headline you feel most uncomfortably comfortable with. Bold wins in today's distracted world. If you aren't bold, you're wasting your time. Turn that negative moment into a year-end victory for your cheering section to celebrate your milestone at the finish line.

- Highlight a business success, team learning, philanthropic impact, quick tweet from the CEO or high- quality picture that tells a powerful story in each section of your company's year-end newsletter.

- Better yet, make a brief highlight video to place on

social media; you can even run some Facebook ads to reinforce your value to your key market and target a diverse demographic you want to pull in. You don't need a million dollars to do this; you need the drive and desire to make your story stand out.

Now you might be thinking, "I'm not a big business. In fact, I'm a real estate agent, and my business is just me." My response to you is this: You are a brand.

People are engaged with you, or they aren't. Your bank account is either in the black or in the red (which should spur you to take critical action). Remember that every single person in this world has an amazing story to tell. Share a side of you that people can relate to, that they'll remember in a positive way. Above all else, think more of yourself and the time you spend doing what you love to do as an entrepreneur by sharing value with your world.

Whether you're a bigger company or someone getting their side hustle on building a business, go big or go home! The choice is up to you. You can roll into another year with the same results, or you can be bold enough to share your year-end headline letting the world know about the hours you put in each day to provide the best service or products to your customers. What's your decision?

EIGHT

CREATING HEALTHY CULTURES TO DRIVE DESIRED OUTCOMES

When asked how people are doing, many reply "I'm busy." Our tech-focused world tied to capitalism's goal of productivity and humans as a resource, is making it hard for a lot of people today. Across generations, people are struggling in answering this simple question, "*How are you doing?*"

While business results must happen, we must remember that humans are at the core of every business from the small shop that employs five people to the international corporation employing 50,000 people.

The gift of being human is having a human spirit that wants to feel a sense of purpose, connection, and support. While the modern day human focuses on technology, there are hardwired primal instincts within us that shape our leadership, culture, and overall health as we adapt to the confines of the material world's need for income to survive.

Being human isn't easy, and being responsible for the lives of other humans as a business leader is even more challenging.

Business leaders are often focused on complex strategies, 30,000 foot views, and forget that life itself is fairly simple when we strip ourselves of titles, ego, and the expectations that we place on ourselves, and in turn, place onto others.

I propose, leadership is quite simple - *it requires us to think less and to act more.* To act in ways that are simple and that are focused on fundamental human needs over intellectual thought.

Why Simple Questions Are Really Hard

Simple questions are really hard to answer today because people's brains are on a hamster wheel spinning around - ping, swipe, like, right? Cognition is the process of acquiring knowledge through thought, experience, and senses. While humans, from a functional level, can process hundreds of things each minute, our soul or spirit cannot. When our mind is jumbled with noise, we lose the depth of our highest consciousness and find it hard to answer meaningful questions deep within our psyche.

Why I Don't Care If You're Busy

Daily, I ask every person before me this one simple question, "How are you doing?" Guess what? Very few respond from their soul, and most, reply with nothing short of what an emoji could tell me - "I'm busy." Digging deeper, I ask, "Does busy mean good or bad?" Sound the privacy invasion alarm! Warning, Warning, Warning, this man before me is now going too deep - deep to a place that I don't even know anymore as I am lost in the grind of life.

Here's why I don't care if you are busy.

Being busy has nothing to do with you! Let me say it again, *being busy has nothing to do with you.*

Busy is a task and by definition it means you're occupied. So occupied in your own thoughts you are unable to connect with a live human being right before you.

Why Busy Isn't an Answer Great Managers Accept

Transactional managers view employees as their greatest cost, so hearing that their people are busy is music to their productive mind.

Transformational managers understand the need for transactional behavior to meet metrics, but dig deeper to understand what motivates, inspires, and drives their greatest assets, people. Great managers will never accept busy for an answer because great managers know the importance of authentic connection.

Great managers understand that people need to pay their bills as adults, yet deep within, is a free spirit who wants to find itself through the facade of corporate dress codes, meeting schedules, and company kool-aide pouring another layer of what to believe onto the human soul. Great managers care about feelings while caring about the task at hand, because feeling drives engagement.

Exceptional managers realize that time is the greatest gift, and for every hour their people are at work under their leadership, they are trading time away from exercise, aging parents, sick children, community issues, social advocacy campaigns, and things more meaningful than the job you provide them. For most, work is work, until people self-actualize passion, talent, skill, and market needs to live life full of vitality - the highest level according to Maslow's hierarchy of needs. Exceptional managers focus on elevating their team members to actualize their highest potential in their work, encouraging collaborative conversations over avoidant words like, busy.

Busy Isn't the Purpose of Life

Authentic managers know one universal truth.

The purpose of life is to learn how to love yourself so you can learn how to love others.

When I work with organizations, we breakdown old beliefs that do not serve employees well while people learn to hold a safe space in meetings by accessing vulnerability, trust, and communication skills. Senior leaders learn from entry level employees and are reminded what it's like starting out while junior employees learn what managers are responsible for on those daily conference calls. In all, we learn that it's vital to our team's success to take a moment answering this not so simple question, "How are you doing?" with a real response so we can support team members wherever they're at on their journey.

Will you take a moment and let me know how you are doing today?

Meeting For Purpose and Clarity in Communication

Oh boy, another meeting. Do you have another meeting coming up or one that you are wondering why you're even there in the first place? Well, you're not alone. According to Doodle's 2019 State of Meetings report, the cost of poorly organized meetings in 2019 will reach $399 billion in the U.S. and $58 billion in the U.K. This is almost half a trillion dollars for these two countries alone! Depending on the surveys you read, over half of respondents feel that meetings are either a distraction, unnecessary, or a waste of time. While it's nice to see people, you need to have a purpose to meet.

Consulting leadership teams to help them improve communications and resource management, I advise that internal meetings need to fall into three categories for Small-Medium sized organizations:

1. Executive Team Meetings (ETM) – In this meeting you need to keep it high-level tracking your performance dashboard. Performance dashboards often provide real time insight into trends like: revenue, membership

growth, customer retention, employee headcount, and major expenses on things like necessary technology improvements to aide in the overall business strategy. Meetings like this should not get into the weeds on an individual employee matter, rather, in this case, they should focus on the type of employee evaluation the organization would like to conduct, it's frequency, and identify key resources while issuing a timeline to complete. If people need to meet, they can meet on specific tasks or set-up follow-up meetings. Keep these meetings focused on the overall business strategy, not the tactics.

2. Staff Meeting (SM) -In this meeting you need to be present as a leader and invite your staff to attend. You can issue survey questions ahead of the meeting to assess data or employee insights so that you are prepared to address any issues or concerns. A benefit of being present as a leader in staff meetings is that your team members will feel a sense of trust as they have the opportunity to share ideas that otherwise would not make their way to the top. You can encourage teamwork by facilitating a question from the group that needs help, and then going rapid-fire around the table having people ask for a team consult. Each team member gets two chances to go and has one-minute to offer quick nuggets of advice or perspective to the employee seeking

help. This keeps things moving so the meeting does not become about one person. Staff meetings can also be themed to have fun; why not make it tropical beach day and serve your staff some Hawaiian appetizers to boost morale.

3. 1:1 or Team Meetings – Are important to keep the cadence and accountability to the team's deliverables. Whether this is between a CEO and CFO or a sales executive and sales manager, these meetings allow people to work on specific, focused work and hash out any details or challenges to minimize the disruption of work. If managers choose to schedule 1:1 meetings, there should be a mutual expectation that the manager offers valuable insight, coaching, and time for questions while their direct report comes prepared with data, next steps, and a solid overview of where they are and where they intend to go while asking for support.

Some general rules to live by to make meetings valuable, include:

- Set clear objectives for your meeting and know your desired outcomes
- Have a clear agenda and stick to it
- Check-in 10 minutes before your meeting ends to ask if anyone has a hard stop if you feel like you are running over, and always let people know that if you

run over it is ok for them to leave; that you will send a re-cap of the meeting via email

- Have the right people in the room
- Use the appropriate technology and make sure everyone knows how to use it before the meeting if you are presenting or asking people to use a platform their organization does not support
- Consider learning styles and have the right mix of videos, PowerPoint, charts, etc. and only use them if they help you achieve your objective
- Give people three options for meeting dates when scheduling
- Never schedule on sacred time like lunches or walking breaks that people use for self-care
- Have a designated person to take notes and ensure a follow-up email is sent with a re-cap, if needed
- Double check time zones for international or domestic meetings across states
- Know what a great meeting looks like for everyone in the room; know what the exchange is for them to be there giving up their time to hear you present
- Never waste people's time, never!
- Always come prepared and remember to make the meeting valuable for everyone while taking care of your objective to achieve your desired outcome
- Practice before your meeting if you are a new

manager or new to presenting so that you keep your words tight and allow time for feedback to let others feel valued

- Effective breakouts need to be managed by one person for every seven people to exercise an effective span of control, either online or in-person; do not let your groups get too big

- Always, Always, stay in command and control of your meeting; do not let it get hijacked!

If you use my advice, you can cut down on endless meetings as you meet with a clear purpose in mind. Utilizing the points listed above, you can create more value for everyone in your meeting so people want to take a meeting with you because of the value you offer!

NINE

UNDERSTANDING IMPORTANT DIFFERENCES TO BE SUCCESSFUL IN TODAY'S GLOBAL ECONOMY

Understanding cultural differences is an essential leadership skill in today's business environment. Whether you're an executive traveling overseas to negotiate a deal, an expat managing a footwear brand's supply chain in a foreign country, or a team member working in an organization that fosters diversity, equity, and inclusion, it's time to up your knowledge and understanding of cultural differences. This culture guide brief provides real world examples of cultural differences so you come across like a cultured individual in today's global business environment.

Ethics is critical to business, yet, ethical beliefs are different across societies because of cultural norms, political ideology, and belief systems.

When I arrived to India, I met a developer who was building schools to get children out of poverty; one of his schools actually sends kids to Harvard, so his model clearly works. Standing in the elevator, he reached into his pocket to show our group stacks of money while telling us that this money was going to be used to pay for the water system for his newest school, and that if he went to the local government for the permitting process, it would take years; worse, the money would not end up in the right place. The question is, is this ethical? Should he go through the government process that would keep kids out of an education and out of a school with running water for years, or should he handle things as he knows in his culture to create the needed change in a country desperate for education at this level to transform human potential?

Take a moment to write your thoughts. What would you do and why would you do it?

_____

_____

_____

_____

_____

_____

Departing India, I set off to another destination, Thailand. Visiting *The Land of Smiles*, one may wonder why there is a picture of a certain man in every local shop and board room of major companies. Well, that picture is The King of Thailand and his image is intended to reflect the country's devotion, loyalty and respect to the monarch. In fact, speaking out about the monarch will get you into big trouble, so don't do it. This is far different from America where memes are generated on social media to make fun of our presidents without repercussion. When you understand Thai culture, you will also understand the importance of reverence, the deep respect for something. This is palpable when you ask for directions or help in Thailand, also known as the land of smiles.

This brings us to the importance of *belief systems*. What you believe in your short time on this planet is not the same as what billions of other humans believe. Our belief systems are shaped by numerous things, including: religion, nationalism, social media, money, education, diversity, travel, mentors, personal relationships, family, security, law, spirituality, lived experiences, political ideology, and more.

We've seen how the American government goes to war when belief systems surrounding political ideology are at play, as was the case for the Vietnam War and longstanding treatment of Cuba. We've also seen how we turn the other cheek as people in Africa are killed daily without much intervention on our behalf. The American belief system, rooted deeply in the belief of freedom and capitalism, also has its challenges.

As American business leaders, we have the choice. We have the choice to re-invest in our communities and we have the choice to make an impact for people we don't know, if we shift our belief from a nation rooted in fierce independence to a progressive social democracy where basic rights like healthcare or housing are afforded. In a nation with so much wealth as America, is it ethical to let those with less suffer because they aren't "strong enough" as other individuals or do we have a social contract to do more?

Venturing to the land down under in Australia, I was shocked at the prices for a meal. $25 for a breakfast? Meeting up with my coffee industry friends, I griped and moaned a bit at the cost of things until I shifted my mindset back to that of the curious traveler, to get out of the *my country* mindset, so I could understand the differences. As a social democracy, you don't see a ton of mentally ill people harassing tourists like you do in downtown San Francisco, and I surely did not see tent cities in the urban core due to Australia's belief in the *tall poppy syndrome*, where hoarding wealth is frowned upon. What I learned is that everyone has access to healthcare; baristas make a living wage where they can buy a home; tips and tax are included; the food is cleaner given the access to quality foods and a smaller population; exercise is reinforced with public pools located on beautiful coastlines; and, their advertising is downright hilarious.

You see, traveling will expose you to learn more about how others think if you put on the *veil of ignorance*.

Returning back to India, I was amazed at the noise, density, and poverty at the same time I was amazed at the energy, community, and vitality. Yin and yang.

Walking down the streets of Mumbai, my paramedic hat went on for a second as I asked "what happens if you need to call 911? I don't see many ambulances nearby or hospitals." My host laughed and said, "Drew, we believe in Hinduism. We believe that this is not the final life, so we do not invest the crazy money you do into healthcare. If something happens you will go to the local clinic and hope they keep you alive in the golden hour. From there, they will get an ambulance and the doctor will go if they can. In America, you believe you only get one life until you go to heaven, so you put a lot of money into staying healthy for this one time. We do not live in the same fear that you do about life and death."

Traveling can be scary for business leaders who have never left the country. They often cling to fear based "facts" that are simply not true. While healthcare is vastly different across each country, developed nations will keep you alive. A great way to look at things is to look at the average life expectancy where you will notice, the United States does not even come close to the Top 10. While Americans live long lives like many developed nations, we are not living healthier lives because, the stress rooted in our belief system, is killing us as we trade off quality time for capitalism's sense of urgency.

Traveling, onward...

I learned from Europeans, who work for some of the same corporations we have in the United States, that they receive one month of holiday time compared to our two week vacation and that father's get paid time to be with their newborn children.

Work is work no matter where you are in the world my friend and time is our greatest gift.

Isn't a salesperson or accountant doing the same thing in France as they do in America? Knowing this made me stronger for my next job as I negotiated from a better lens and it made me think differently as a leader helping CEOs build cultures that are truly healthier, for employees and their family members who need quality time at home. Again, understanding why we believe what we believe and question if it is the healthiest choice, is one of the healthiest things we can do, leveraging the gift of cultures to spur innovative workplace practices.

Holding hands with another man, I was walked across the frenzy of a busy Indian street. Back at home, people would have mixed emotions, while in India, it is perfectly normal to see men holding hands as they walk the town showcasing genuine care.

Grabbing a cup of coffee with my Brazilian friends at a coffee conference, I offered the standard American greeting of a handshake and was also given the unique Brazilian greeting of a light kiss on each cheek. Whoa! Hold it, a kiss? Yes, it is harmless, yet if one does not know about things like this, or if it is the first time, things may arise like "oh no, my wife is going to kill me!" Well, your wife might kill you, but just know this is perfectly normal in Brazilian culture and no way does it seek to destroy your personal relationship.

Reading is key to becoming a well-informed business leader, and knowing the works of Geert Hofstede is critical to doing business abroad or managing teams from different cultures. Hofstede's theory identified six dimensions of culture, which are: power distance, individualism vs. collectivism, uncertainty avoidance, masculinity vs. femininity, short-term vs. long-term orientation, and indulgence vs. self-restraint.

From a management perspective, it is important to know about these areas. You can compare countries to learn more about each culture in order to have effective communication across multi-cultural teams. From a sales perspective, you can also learn how to sell into other markets as you take the time to understand their culture.

In looking at the Power Distance below, we see Saudi Arabia ranks high, meaning people are largely uncomfortable speaking directly to authority and may be limited in their ability to offer direct criticism, compared to their American counterpart, who has a lower Power Distance ranking, making them more comfortable with challenging authority.

In looking at masculine vs. feminine values, this research compares a nation's driver of competition vs. care. When we look at South Korea, we learn that Koreans value quality of life in comparison to Americans, who value independence and standing out from the crowd.

Long-term orientation is also driven by a nation's collective values system, and we see that in Asia, where there is more focus on steady long-term growth compared to quarterly results that must be delivered in American businesses that report to Wall Street.

This country comparison chart, found on www.Hofstede-Insights.com provides a comparative example of cultural differences that lead to the culture and norms of one's society.

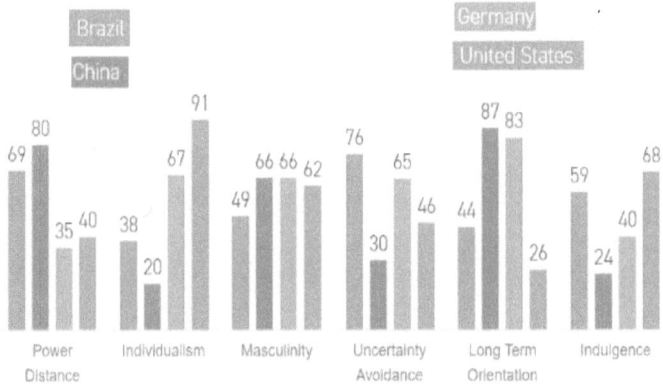

While managers use numerous tools like DiSC assessments for sales teams, it is critical that global managers learn how to use this information to develop high-performing multi-cultural teams. While the challenges of running a global business can be tough, today it is easier to understand our differences and ways we can learn about each other to have rewarding relationships aligned with our goals.

I hope my stories and context helped you understand the value of our connected world, the power of belief systems, and the need to spark a conversation within your circle on ways you can seek to understand others at a higher level instead of reacting with biased views.

Ultimately, there are billions of people on this planet with different beliefs in our limited time that we are here, so do you, and get to know why other people think what they think. You'll be surprised at the growth you'll achieve as a leader with this approach to understanding other humans!

TEN

BUILDING AN EMPLOYEE HAPPINESS PROGRAM

Research shows that 67% of employees are not engaged in their work and 18% are actively disengaged in their work. This happens at leading companies, the one's with big brand logos you know to local mom and pop shops. While there are many reasons why employees are not engaged, one thing that employers can do is work on driving employee happiness.

Can money buy happiness?

Research has shown that money only makes people happy for so long. While everyone needs a basic level of income to feel secure with the requirements of taxes, rent or mortgage payments, student loans, rising healthcare costs, etc. they also need to feel a sense of purpose within their day to day life to feel happy and connected to what they're doing.

With changing demographics in the workforce, younger generations are also demanding more experiences and better work-life integration because they are connected 24/7 to company emails. The standard labor law dictating full-time employment at 40 hours per week is due for an overhaul, as this system is not geared towards the needs of many salaried individuals or hourly workers that make up the majority of professional services careers today. Granted, certain roles like nursing or assembly line work requires physical presence, there are many avenues to build flexibility into the modern-day workplace to drive employee happiness.

Cultures that build self-esteem through psychologically safe management approaches encourage the development of a human's full potential; they also foster a culture to continuously learn on personal and professional levels.

After college, people are still curious, they want to learn, and they want to acquire new knowledge or skills. Beyond the annual sales training or mandated training, you can build programs that encourage personal development over professional development to build happy individuals who are more self-aware; in turn, this builds better teams that are mindful in communication and better managers who avoid projection to stay grounded in truth.

Free time is a necessity to feeling alive and working on personal goals.

While you offer company provided cell phones as a -perk of employment or vehicles with tracking devices tied to productivity software, smart employees know these are not perks or true benefits, they are tools of management to drive profitability through productivity metrics. Beyond tools to do the job, the most valuable gift we have in life is time. Time allows us to write books, time to spend uninterrupted moments with our children, and time to know ourselves at a deeper level through journaling, counseling, coaching, or other methods of self- improvement.

So, how do you get more time or give people more time?

Studies have shown that employees spend hours throughout the work week surfing social media and not being productive. Simply put, they are punching the clock because our system tied to labor law and benefits makes them do jobs to get basic benefits in our society; for those who are overly productive or highly efficient, they are often told to slow down to stay at the same pace as the group to stay on-point within the confines of the system.

People who are highly productive, efficient, direct in communication, and LEAN in their methodology to getting to the desired outcome are often met with resistance from bureaucratic consensus seekers who can stall projects because these people find ways to waste time, adhering to what's prescribed by the system, filling their time with endless meetings that lead to the same lackluster outcomes. Time gets wasted on a daily basis, in mass quantity that amounts to billions in revenue, because of poor leadership and managers who are not empowered to make decisions. Worse, time is spent being busy when wages are stagnant and American workers are spending less quality time at home on important needs like raising their children, aka our next-generation workforce, and are spending more time being busy.

Remember, there's a difference between the quantity you work and the quality of the work you produce.

While it's great to think every employee wants to be at work, the reality is that a large percentage would rather be doing things they loved. This is hard to accept as an entrepreneur because your passion got you here; realize though, most people will not be in leadership roles like you, and that many more simply need a job to make it through life as they find their purpose.

Think about your vacation policies, value-adds like giving employees paid time-off to volunteer for their favorite non-profit, early-release days for admin staff, work from home flexibility to avoid major commute times, and ensuring your talent has quality time with their children and significant other. Time matters and giving time is a leadership choice.

Management is a philosophy.

I believe in letting hourly workers take off a few hours early on a Friday if they've done their job; I've even answered the phone as the receptionist a few times when I knew I had work to do and when I knew the receptionist didn't, taking a leadership position that gave that person time to do whatever they wanted while receiving their full salary.

When we focus on the purpose of our work and the desired outcome as the goal, we realize that there are weeks when we have 70 hours of work to do and weeks when we have 20 to 30 hours of work to do. This is perplexing in office environments when some people are salaried and other people reporting to them are classified as hourly; this doesn't make sense if you want to build a purpose driven culture.

While roles like graphic design can be hourly or project based using freelancers, certain core office jobs, if re-classified, would serve organizations much better and the people employed. When you ask most hourly employees if they want to leave early and when their benefits are tied to certain hours, the result will be no, even if the truthful answer is yes. This type of management system is archaic and ripe for change.

Trading time in one place to get to another matters.

Outsourcing projects is a way to free up time if you are a small business owner or entrepreneur. Sites like www.Fiverr.com allow you to hire peer reviewed freelancers who post their portfolios for your review before hiring them on a project basis, or fee for service.

Time is money.

If you can pay someone $250 to make a logo and this frees up two days of work for you to network and drive product sales generating $1000, then this is a good reason to outsource as you exchange money for more time to make more money!

From a management standpoint, giving up control is necessary if you want to have more time to focus on strategy. Outsourcing is also effective to take pressure off of your team members if they are busy and focused on projects. When working with CEOs I always encourage them to have a priority list of projects that staff are working on to show the Board. From there, I help them explain options to board members when they want to add more projects, that the options are: identifying which project they want to remove in order to add this one given staff resources, or asking for money and resources to outsource X need while staff executes what has already been planned. Effective management involves effective choices.

The choices you make and the way you think define your outcomes.

Research shows that between 60-80% of human thought is negative depending on the study you read; that over 80% of our thoughts get repeated if we do not actively work on eliminating negative thought patterns. This is a reason why so many homes are negative and filled with divorce and why some corporate cultures are defined as toxic workplaces by employees sharing their pain on sites like Glassdoor.

As a leader, you set the tone, you set the stage for a happy work environment or a negative environment rooted in pessimistic thinking. The choice is yours to begin developing healthy cultures as you create more psychological awareness around your own thoughts, projections, and treatment of others you lead.

While employees spend the majority of their adult life in the workplace, it is up to leaders to challenge our system to get better benefits for our talent, to create healthier office environments to reduce the healthcare outcomes we see today, and to support the whole person.

Employee happiness starts with happy leaders who are connected to mind, body, and spirit while leading team members in the pursuit of business goals.

I encourage leaders to use technology or monthly surveys to keep an eye on employee happiness. Don't be afraid to ask your employees what they think of their benefits packages, how they'd like to use a company sponsored day off with pay, and what food they'd like to see in the office at your next meeting. It's the little things that lead to long- term loyalty.

Human-Centered Leadership Questions

Now that we've covered some management philosophy and the importance of relating to others across cultures, take a moment to reflect and answer these question, as honest as you can.

Is business responsible for solving some of the challenges society faces today? Why or why not?

_____

_____

_____

_____

_____

What are challenges that your organization can get more
involved with on a local, state, or federal level?

_____

_____

_____

_____

_____

_____

_____

How can your involvement on this cause serve as a positive
reflection of your company's mission and your purpose as a
leader?

_____

_____

_____

_____

_____

_____

_____

What unconscious bias do you have towards other humans of a different race, religion, or background? How does this show up in your life?

_____

_____

_____

_____

_____

_____

_____

What is one actionable step that you can do to begin learning about people who are different than you, starting this week?

_____

_____

_____

_____

_____

_____

_____

How can your workplace better meet the needs to support the realities of many employees who face challenges, from student loan debt to living paycheck to paycheck to healthcare costs, etc.?

_____

_____

_____

_____

_____

_____

_____

_____

_____

_____

_____

_____

_____

_____

_____

_____

ELEVEN

NETWORKING TIPS TO MAXIMIZE YOUR OPPORTUNITIES

After a career ending injury as a firefighter, I took what I knew about people, community, and connection into business. I also sought out opportunities to learn from others, including leaders, CEOs, and people whose work I admired. Believing in the old truth that life is more about who you know than what you know, I joined LinkedIn and grew my personal brand and network to over 10,000 people. Networking has given me a robust relationship bank that I can leverage to help people or call on when I need help. I encourage everyone to network, even though it may seem awkward at first, because this world offers so much when we are brave enough to ask for help, ask for guidance, and ask someone for their perspective to help us grow.

The following are my Top 10 Tips to help you network...

1. Be Yourself

In life, there are people who genuinely care about you and they are your ride or die crew until the end. Then, there are people who are for whatever cause you are for at any given time in life, and the other are the people who are for whatever it is you are opposed to in life at any given time. You attract different people into your network as you evolve and you will attract the best people once you learn to show-up 100% as your authentic, genuine self.

2. Know Your Talent

In my faith, we talk about spiritual gifts and unique talents as a blessing. Understand what your special talent(s) is and harness it to its fullest potential. Some of us are great leaders, managers, teachers, care takers, advocates, photographers, writers, etc. Know what you are good at and dive deeper into your gift to see if you can combine business and your talent. People love passionate, knowledgeable people, so don't be surprised when you attract interested people who want to know you at a deeper level. And on a money-making note, the future of our workforce will be highly specialized, so get in early and develop your talent!

3. Diversify Your Network

In life and business, we are all interconnected. I've seen companies struggle time and time again via death by vertical where information does not transfer over and time is wasted trying to replicate things when solutions are readily available. Diversify your network and meet other leaders or managers in industries that are outside of your norm. Chances are you'll learn that there might be ways to collaborate on things to help your organization grow.

4. Join a Committee or Board

Building on network diversification, serving on a board or executive committee is a great way to meet other people who are genuinely engaged in life and business. These people are seeking ways to find solutions vs. others who might be more problem focused using up hours of life on wasted emotion. You do not have to be a CEO to serve on a board or executive committee, but you do have to have the courage to know your worth and to ask your senior leaders if they will sponsor you as a representative. Joining boards is also a great way to earn trust with C-level leaders to build lasting partnerships if you are in a sales role...

5. Don't Sell People Stuff, Deliver Value

I get hit up on the daily with canned email responses from people who know nothing about me or what I do. If you send things to people, have an understanding of their role, if they can make a decision, and if your offering is relevant to them. If you have a 10X solution per your generic message without a website and client testimonials, good luck! People who make decisions want to know how you can help them, what results you've delivered, and why you are interested in their organization. One of the biggest deals I closed was through #4 above and by delivering value across every touch point from the initial email through negotiating terms. Remember, it is about your customer, not your sales quota.

6. Be Mindful of Your Platform

There is a difference when you have 500 of your closest customers and friends on LinkedIn to hosting the equivalent of a small town like I do today with 10,000 followers. When I worked for a global brand, my mentor gave me this advice "While your boss wants X and is saying this, the company needs this and is doing this." There is a big difference in your wants at a local level and the needs of a larger platform. We all want to share things in today's digital era, so ask yourself, do you need to share this before you post it and how will your message impact those who read it. Today, we are drowning in an information overload with endless scrolls. As your platform evolves, your message may need to be broader. You can still use a local photo from a local event, just be sure to craft a bigger narrative on how this impacts leadership or society as a whole. Be mindful of your platform and the impact your communication has on others.

7. See Who Viewed You

In the settings section on LinkedIn you can opt to let others see that you viewed their profile or be the mysterious person who creeps on profiles not showing your face. The reason why I prefer showing my profile is that in return, I can see when others have viewed my profile. Typically, I send them a connection request. Don't overthink connecting. If they viewed you, there's a reason why, so why not connect? If they don't accept, keep it moving!

8. Build Your Own Website

Securing your name online is important today because it is the first thing that shows up in a Google search. I always advise clients who are on the leadership track to secure their first and last name via sites like www.GoDaddy.com While you don't have to use it right away, you have it for the time when you are ready to launch your book, product, or run for office. Reputation management is key to growing and building your brand. Build your own website to let others see your portfolio and aspects of your life that you like to feature. When you search on sites like www.Google.com you will see that personal websites and LinkedIn links are at the top. Claim your name and build a fun site today!

9. Show Up Strong

Networking events can be stressful even to the most experienced networkers. We are all running fast in today's connected society, from meeting to meeting or family health issue to the boardroom, time waits for no one. When you meet others for the first time, first impressions matter and they do count to how people perceive you psychologically. If you know you are not at your best and need to do some self-care, that is more important than showing up to an event in a panic attack. Show up strong, cut out the excessive drinking just to fit in, be mindful of others, listen more than you talk by asking the right questions, and be yourself.

10. Enjoy What You Do

My network is amazing! I get to see people from Google testing autonomous vehicles to organic food brands changing the way we think about food to elected officials shaping the landscape of our nation. In every group, I see people who truly enjoy what they are doing and it shows. If you are in flux or not enjoying your work, spend some time with a recruiter and explore the different jobs, cultures, and sizes of organizations out there until you find your fit. Remember, you are never too old to start something new or to learn something. The challenging times plant the seeds for our growth and through faith, we continue moving forward until we find the next thing we enjoy doing.

Keep moving and keep growing! I hope my Top 10 Tips help you or someone you know grow their network to find meaningful connections and conversations in order to make a positive impact as business leaders today!

TWELVE

BUSINESS IN A POST-COVID WORLD

COVID-19 shocked the global economy as the virus made its way around the world. Life, as billions knew it changed in the matter of days, then months.

While America was nearing 3% unemployment in metro regions seeing one of the strongest economies in history, the booming economy suddenly shifted to seeing a record number of unemployment claims topping 30 million a few months after the national emergency was declared. In short, COVID-19 exposed the harsh realities that millions of Americans face and that millions more would face, including: fear of housing security, fear of savings running out, fear of paying student loan debt with no end in sight, fear of healthcare costs, fear of going to work in unhealthy environments, and fear of death causing everyone to face the reality of our own mortality and why we exist – some fears, that are shaped by the very business decisions we make as leaders on a daily basis.

"Be the Change You Wish To See In the World"

– Mahatma Gandhi

During the COVID-19 response, I witnessed many things from my perspective across business to public safety. What I realized early on, is that those in charge of preparedness were not quite prepared for the realities COVID-19 presented. From a leadership perspective I also saw heroic leadership and political games through the use of rhetoric.

From a business perspective, I saw how ill prepared our federal, state, and local governments were prepared when it came to procurement, but most importantly, their lack of knowledge on how business works in the global economy as government agencies seized valuable products redirecting them under wartime measures. Overall, there were numerous learning lessons for business leaders in today's global business environment, which if learned, can help you increase business performance in our post-COVID world and make our society better.

Lesson 1: Debt vs. Cash Flow

America is a debt heavy society where people take on mortgages they may or may not be able to afford; car payments; institutional indentured servitude through the form of student loans financing some degree programs that don't produce a positive ROI; and small business loans to entrepreneurs who have no business acumen or safety net given the reality of small business failure rates.

The debt schemes in America are heavily marketed using behavioral science and marketing psychology to keep people consuming, even if they need to be saving. From in- app purchases linked to stored credit card accounts or traditional advertising, America has made its place as number one in capitalism as a result of spending, including debt.

The debt load many Americans carry is not healthy, nor are the policies around this issue.

Through poor public policy programs, we've seen housing prices and rent rise in urban cores as elected officials cater to overseas investors, aka luxury buildings, that artificially drive up market prices as they displace loyal locals forcing them to commute hours each day. In the end, a basic safety net like housing becomes a burden; it also becomes a burden to many employers who find it tough to staff restaurants and fill entry level retail jobs to keep their debt heavy business venture alive – the point is, we are all interconnected, and so are our decisions when it comes to public policy. While you might not think business has a role in solving these issues, business is truly the lifeblood of America and the biggest platform we have to drive change.

Perspective is everything, and COVID-19 forced people to change their perspective.

Living in Asia taught me the difference between the credit card lifestyle and the cash economy where credit cards are almost useless – that saying cash is king rings true!

Cash flow is the ability to have positive cash on hand and to be liquid during times of crisis. It does you no good to be in a nice home that is financed when the loss of a job comes. While we can put 10% down for a home in America, there are many countries that require a much higher down payment because they know the reality, that one must have good cash flow to weather financial storms caused by layoffs or unthinkable health issues like cancer.

COVID-19 exposed the harsh reality the millions of Americans are one paycheck away from zero cash flow, including those with heavily financed degrees sitting right next to you in your office with a VP title.

As business leaders, it's important to get behind programs that increase the cash flow and savings so your employees can have a bright future; and, in conjunction with 401K plans, offer them with a reputable financial advisor who can have 1:1 meetings with employees to help them achieve a sound retirement; for companies employing people with advanced degrees, also consider the debt that many of your talented hires are in who quite frankly, did not need that extra degree to be the superstar they have always been with specific training and on-the-job mentoring.

While good businesses have good cash flow, making sure that your employees have good cash flow is key. A great way to ensure this is to get involved on political issues from housing to healthcare and public policy think-tanks. Don't leave it up for the Amazon's of the world to shape the policies at play – remember, *small-medium sized businesses are the core and backbone of the American economy.* It's time to make your voice heard to have a sustainable future after the years of hard work put-in.

Lesson 2: Supply Chain

President Donald Trump minced words with the CEO of 3M Company who manufactures the bulk of the world's N-95 masks used by healthcare workers and other industrial workers abroad. While the 3M Company is based in the Midwest region of the United States, the company did what many global corporations do – they offshored a bulk of their manufacturing.

Under the Defense Production Act (DPA), President Trump authorized the federal government's ability to control manufacturing efforts; furthermore, medical imports from China were seized by federal authorities, redirecting supplies to essential services or the national stockpile.

These situations brought up a major reality concerning our supply chain.

After traditional supply chain resources were exhausted from corporate channels, those seeking supplies had to rely on tertiary supply chains from business people who have networks and the know-how to procure reputable goods abroad for export.

Through the initial crisis, we learned that there is not a thorough knowledge of global resources and a streamlined approach to mass procurement and distribution for a national emergency. We also learned that we put all of our eggs in one basket, and did not diversify our supply chain enough given geo-political threats as the potential for a new world order plays out in our lifetime between the U.S. and China. From a business standpoint, it is essential for you to have a reliable supply chain and a backup to ensure business continuity. Think about your sourcing and diversify in order to stay fluid if trade issues transpire, which, inevitably they will give geo-politics.

Lesson 3: Leveraging Technology

Companies were forced to get with the times overnight as policy leaders enacted swift changes to how business as usual could be carried out. Companies in Silicon Valley, that are technology-forward, had little trouble adapting to this sudden change while many legacy companies across industries found it extremely difficult to shift their workforce from office setting to home office.

Companies that refused to innovate, that refused to give employees the choice to work from home, and that were stuck in their ways were suddenly unstuck.

Humbled by this reality, companies learned many things, including:

1. They can hire talented people outside of state boundaries because commutes are a non-issue; the talent pool widened.

2. Their employees are trustworthy and can carry out the same level of high performance in their homes.

3. Many employees are relieved to not be forced into long, arduous commutes trying to earn a paycheck.

4. Families have more time together at home, which is a great thing for the next-generation of our workforce.

5. The power of choice builds employee loyalty.

6. CEOs had the time to get with the times in order to evolve in our digital era.

7. Work can now be measured by the desired outcome over the desired time seeing employees punch the clock, especially in the professional services field.

8. There are numerous technology solutions available to stay connected, productive, and get results.

9. Cost vs. Benefit analysis were done on real estate assets and what their future use looks like, or if they are even needed in the first place.

10. How people learn and how they can support their talent in this new era.

The forced technological revolution helped many companies improve their workplace as they provided their employees choice, new tools, and the ability to work from home.

Lesson 4: Data Privacy

While technology is great, it also comes with a new set of risks that employers need to take into account. Data privacy is a major risk that companies need to understand today. As my colleague joked, -scammers now have a full- time job since no one can leave home under COVID-19 orders.∥ And, while he joked, the scammers went to work creating engineered phishing scams, phone scams using government names on caller ID, and hacking sites showing how vulnerable we are to data breaches. While those in government know the reality of cyber warfare, most civilians think their technology company protects them; this, a false illusion. The reality is, if people want to hack you, odds are, if they're professionals, they can hack you in some sort of fashion.

That said...

I encourage every business owner to consult with trusted professionals in data privacy, many of whom are cyber security experts with law enforcement, legal, or military backgrounds. These experts can give you advice on your online vulnerabilities and provide steps to secure your virtual business environment to keep it safe.

Defense in the online environment is the best offense.

Data privacy is also important if you run a small business or non-profit that receives protected health information (PHI) because this information is protected by federal law. Take the time to understand what data you hold, why people might want to steal your data, what you can do to protect it, and what legal consequences are out there if something goes wrong.

As we shift from more secured offices to home offices, companies need to invest in this level of security and employee training to minimize risk.

Lesson 5: Leveraging Your Network in Tough Times

One of my coaching clients lost his job, no fault of his own, as the industry he worked in closed down; at the same time, he received a letter for divorce. Supporting multiple children on his sole salary, this was devastating.

He called me up and asked if I would coach him during this time as I did before, helping him triple his salary.

We worked together to put an action plan into place, quickly, as there was no time to waste. Getting his mindset on point after these devastating blows, he was in the right mindset to move forward despite the pain from these losses. Polishing his resume, I asked him if it would be ok to post his story and resume on my LinkedIn platform, something I rarely do for clients. Given the situation with COVID-19, he was running out of options on places to sleep as his savings were exhausted.

A few days later, someone on my network reached out and offered to pay for his hotel; next, he offered to give him a job.

Talking it through with my client and his generous sponsor, he accepted his offer of employment.

This example highlights the power of your network and that anything is truly possible if you are humble enough to ask for help. Beyond the people you know, there is a network of people who want to help. Put yourself out there, put your product out there, and don't worry about the haters. Focus on the good that is truly out there in this world and show-up strong in everything you do!

Your network is bigger and more powerful than you know. Know how and when to leverage it for the right reasons to allow success to flow your way.

BONUS LEADERSHIP ADVICE

America is hurting. This was evident as riots raged across America and people took to social media, either offering words of encouragement or words of outrage across every race, political party, and socioeconomic background.

Calculated responses were drawn up from expensive PR firms echoing almost the same tone and rhetoric, some because they cared, and others because the felt called to join their peers.

Facts were checked and numerous companies who claimed to support equity were blatantly called out for not posting a single woman or minority to their C-Suite. Facts and data do not lie.

This opportunity presented the catalyst for change and for tough conversations to take place; conversations that were long overdue, as demonstrated by the echo chamber of pain from CEOs to people being released from prison trying to find a job.

Leaders, from that moment in history forward, were presented with the opportunity to change with the times or defend the past.

Emotional intelligence comes to play.

We saw the difference between reactive leaders and responsive leaders. We saw the difference between compassionate leaders and authoritarian leaders. We saw the difference between those who want to evolve and those who will defend anything at any cost. We saw the difference between politicians who try and politicians who try to stage photo ops, including both parties to keep their polling results strong. We saw massive amounts of courage and we saw massive amounts of cowardness. We saw humans who uplift the human spirit and we saw humans who kill the human spirit. We saw the difference between emotion without intelligence and intelligence without emotion.

In the end, there were many leadership lessons on emotional intelligence.

As a leader, you can reflect on times of crisis to see how you respond or if you react. You can strive to seek to understand or always make your voice heard. Ultimately, you can learn from challenging moments to become a better version of yourself and leader who is committed to making a positive impact as you grow your business now!

COVID-19 Leadership Questions

Leaders were faced with numerous challenges throughout the initial and ongoing COVID-19 pandemic. Challenges, as you know, can make or break people and they truly define leaders vs. managers. The following questions are designed

to help you go deep as a leader so that you can use this experience to reflect, refine, and redefine your leadership to move your organization forward to meet the needs of the future. Take a moment to read each question and journal in the space provided.

Q1. Did your business have a business continuity or resiliency plan in place in the event of an unforeseen incident?

_____

_____

_____

_____

_____

_____

_____

_____

Q2. What lessons did you learn about your business?

_____

_____

_____

_____

_____

_____

_____

Q3. What lessons did you learn about technology?

_____

_____

_____

_____

_____

_____

_____

_____

Q4. What lessons did you learn about humans and our society?

_____

_____

_____

_____

_____

_____

_____

_____

Q5. How do you see your business doing more to address the challenges that are internal and the challenges that are external in your community?

_____

_____

_____

_____

_____

_____

_____

SELF-REFLECTION

Take a moment to write down what you've learned, how you will apply it, and set a timeframe to put this into action to Grow It Now!

_____

_____

_____

_____

_____

_____

_____

BONUS TIP

Above everything, focus on building your inner-strength and looking after your mind, body, and spirit. While networks can come and go just like a great job, you truly are 100% special and valuable to this world. Do you!

FOLLOW-UP COACHING

While we've covered a lot in this book, there are more resources and insights I would love to share with you to help you Grow It Now! As a coach, I help leaders grow business development opportunities, strategic marketing plans, employee engagement, sales training, and overall strategies to help them actualize their full potential connecting the dots.

I'm grateful that you gave me your time reading my book - in exchange for your time, I am offering a FREE 15 Minute conversation to explore what's possible and if there's a way I can help you grow. To take advantage of this, schedule a call with me at www.DrewAversa.com today!

Business Ideas and Next Steps

www.ingramcontent.com/pod-product-compliance
Lightning Source LLC
Chambersburg PA
CBHW021418210526
45463CB00001B/427